THE LIFE AND TIMES OF

AL CAPONE

Tom Stockdale

CHELSEA HOUSE PUBLISHERS

Philadelphia

First published in traditional hardback edition
©1998, 2001 by Chelsea House Publishers, a subsidiary of
Haights Cross Communications.
Printed in Hong Kong
Copyright © Parragon Book Service Ltd 1995
Unit 13–17, Avonbridge Trading Estate, Atlantic Road
Avonmouth, Bristol, England BS11 9QD

Illustrations courtesy of Hulton Deutsch Collection;
Peter Newark's American Pictures

Library of Congress Cataloging-in-Publication Data
Stockdale, Tom.
    The life and times of Al Capone / by Tom Stockdale.
      p.   cm.
    Originally published: London: Parragon Books, 1996.
    Includes index.
    Summary: A biography of the notorious Chicago gangster
who ruled bootlegging, prostitution, and gambling industries in
the 1920s.
    ISBN 0-7910-4638-9 (hc)
    1. Capone, Al, 1899-1947—Juvenile literature. 2. Criminals—
Illinois—Chicago—Biography—Juvenile literature. 3. Organized
crime—Illinois—Chicago—History—Juvenile literature.
[1. Capone, Al, 1899-1947. 2. Criminals.]   I. Title.
HV6248.C17S76 1997
364.1'092—dc21
[B]   97-26029
                                           CIP
                                         AC

CONTENTS

Al Capone

The hard-eyed, heavy-set figure of Al Capone stands as the embodiment of gangster rule. His name is a worldwide symbol of lawlessness, and the years since his domination of late-1920s Chicago have given his career a romantic edge. Hollywood has glamorized gangsters in general, and Capone in particular, in films featuring charismatic lead actors like James Cagney *(Angels with Dirty Faces)* and Robert De Niro *(The Untouchables)*. In 1989 there was a serious, though unsuccessful, proposal to make Capone's Chicago home a historic landmark.

Yet Capone's rule over the Chicago area lasted for not much more than five years (1925 to 1931), though it was a period marked by ruthless violence and murder. His rise to power and control of the Chicago gangs paid no heed to innocent lives, and Capone himself maintained his reputation by personal, as well as delegated, killing of his enemies. He displayed a calculated, perverse logic in his attitude to his calling, describing himself as a businessman; the fact that his "business" had its origins in illegal activities and used the methods of warfare was a logical if dirty consequence.

Al Capone's life and career would not have had such an effect on the world had it not been for two outside factors. One was the history and nature of the city he came to dominate, the other a unique American federal law that was almost made to be broken. The history of Chicago was steeped in corruption and law-breaking, and the change in the American Constitution that made business sense out of criminal opportunity was Prohibition, ushered in by the Volstead Prohibition Act (passed in 1919), which made the sale or consumption of alcoholic liquor illegal throughout the United States.

Big Jim Colosimo

THE MAKING OF A MOBSTER

When Gabriel Capone brought his young family from Naples to New York in 1893, he was following a trend that filled the city with unskilled labor from all over Europe. They came to escape a bleak rural life in the promise of work and success in the brave new world of post–Civil War America. By 1910, 11 percent of New York's population was of Italian origin. In most cases the immigrants found only a harsh urban existence, with poor pay and cramped conditions.

Gabriel had been educated in Italy, and his literacy enabled him to avoid the slave labor of manual work. He was soon able to afford the rent on premises in which to practice his profession; he was a barber, and a crowded city provided enough customers for the family to escape from the lowest levels of poverty. Theresa Capone, Gabriel's wife, gave birth to their fourth son on January 17, 1899. Like his brothers he was given an Italian name, but unlike them his did not need to be Americanized. Alphonsus Capone grew up in the mean area around the naval dockyard, in a four-room apartment where Theresa would give birth to another five children. In 1907 the family moved to the Italian district of South Brooklyn.

The Italian New Yorkers came from a country used to the tyranny of foreign invasion, and the children of the immigrants grew up on the streets of a city where gangs continued the regional and national rivalries of their mother

John Torrio

countries. Al carried on an irregular school education until he was fourteen; the streets provided a parallel classroom, offering a more physical curriculum, although his better-than-average school grades showed he had a quick mind.

By the time he was eleven, he was a member of one of the junior gangs that taught its members the arts of petty vandalism and brawling in preparation for the more serious misdeeds of the seniors. Al was big for his age, and quickly asserted himself as a hot-headed member of the Forty Thieves Juniors, an off-shoot of the adult Five Points gang.

Paul Kelly, the leader of the 1500-strong Five Points, combined crime and culture, running gambling houses and brothels and attending the opera with all the trappings of a gentleman. He took under his wing John Torrio, a minor gang leader whose mental capabilities made up for his lack of brawn. Under Kelly's tutelage Torrio gained the reputation of a rational criminal in the irrational underworld; when he could, he kept the peace by negotiation, but when words were not enough his violence was clinical. Al Capone was too young to come under Torrio's influence in New York, but in 1909 the twenty-seven-year-old Torrio set their paths on a converging course when he transferred to Chicago to assist gang boss Big Jim Colosimo against some rivals who were trying to extort money from him.

By the time he was fourteen, Capone was an experienced street fighter and had learned how to use a knife and a gun. His schooling finally ended when he assaulted his teacher in the classroom. Thereafter he took to the life of the streets, earning a few honest dollars in a factory and a book bindery, and becoming a proficient pool player.

He was introduced to the senior Five Points gang by his first mentor, a Brooklyn hoodlum and friend of John Torrio named Frankie Yale, who installed the thickset teenager as barman and bouncer at his bar and brothel, the Harvard Inn. At sixteen Capone was helping to control Yale's prostitution, gambling, extortion, and protection rackets, both physically and administratively. Yale fostered in Capone the intelligent use of violence, for the youngster could not always see that talk was often cheaper for business.

It was at the Harvard Inn during 1917 that Capone got into a fight that gave rise to his nickname, Scarface. Though he later told a story involving shrapnel wounds received during the First World War, it was in fact the result of a clumsy attempt to chat up the young sister of a small-time criminal, Frank Galluccio. Unaware of a family connection, Capone insulted Galluccio's honor with his comments, and before he could settle the resulting argument with a knockout punch, received three everlasting knife-cut reminders of his false move. One was from ear to mouth, one on the jaw, and the third on the neck. His lucky escape cost him thirty stitches. The adversaries were made to apologize to each other, and Capone returned to his duties after a hard-won lesson in the importance of thought before action.

By the following year Capone had a couple of murders under his belt and had escaped prosecution due to loss of evidence and the conveniently bad memories of witnesses. He was rising in the estimation of his fraternity when he met and fell in love with Mae Coughlin, an Irish girl two years his senior. Their first son, Albert (always called Sonny), was born shortly before their marriage in December 1918, and the future seemed set for the family in New York. An outburst of temper changed everything during the following year.

Arthur Finnegan, an Irish gang member, took to insulting Italians in a bar where Capone was taking a drink. Capone beat the offensive Irishman to within an inch of his life, and soon heard that the gang was seeking revenge. Frankie Yale decided it was best for his protégé to lie low for a while, and arranged with John Torrio for Capone to spend some time in Chicago. It was to be an eventful stay.

Prostitution had made a rich man out of Big Jim Colosimo. It had also made him a target for the so-called Black Handers, who extorted money from the wealthy by death threats. This was the reason John Torrio had been transferred from New York to Chicago, where his speedy dispatch of several of the extortionists relieved Colosimo of his problem, and Big Jim persuaded Torrio to stay on. Torrio's efficiency and reputation soon brought him his own "business" opportunities, as well as a cut of Colosimo's take.

Chicago was a town set up for corruption. From the 1830s its multitude of gambling dens and brothels earned it the title of "wickedest city in the United States." Law enforcement was enmeshed in the profits of these activities from this time, and police bribery was seen as a normal business expense. The city's public officials made no secret of their affiliation with criminals; indeed, such links helped to bring victory in the polls, from a populace that cherished Chicago's open-house tradition of vice. "Chicago is unique," admitted one honest council member. "It is the only completely corrupt city in America." In a town full of bribes received and favors owing, youth, intelligence, and immorality were a winning combination.

Of course, there were some honest public servants, and every so often there was a crackdown on crime, when brothels would be closed and minor gangsters arrested, especially after the killing of a policeman or other public servant. But Big Jim Colosimo and John Torrio never spent more than a few hours in jail, for they were greasing palms higher up in the machine than the station house. By the time Al Capone arrived in the city in 1919, Colosimo and Torrio were rich enough to be running their seedier brothels and bars around safe areas in the suburbs, while keeping prestigious, near-legitimate premises in the city.

Torrio gave Capone his first position in the Four Deuces, a four-story building with all the vices under one roof that also served as Torrio's headquarters. Capone soon showed his new boss that he was a cut above the normal hoodlum, creating a front for himself as an antiques dealer, while the additional advantage of having the recommendation of

Frankie Yale brought him into Torrio's confidence. Torrio could make good use of smart assistance, for his sights were set on an entirely new business venture.

By 1919 the advance of the Anti-Saloon League, a powerful temperance organization, had prompted thirty-six of the then forty-eight American states to pass prohibition laws, giving a majority that would make the prohibition of liquor federal law the next year. But Torrio understood full well the difference between the extreme morality of the League, and the more moderate wish of the general public simply to tidy up the seedier incidence of alcohol consumption. He also saw the difficulties in enforcing a law that would be willingly broken, and the ease of buying off the officers charged with such enforcement. Prohibition was a racketeer's dream.

By January 16, 1920, when the Volstead Act became law, warehouses had already been looted and breweries set up as part of Torrio's plan to supply bars with about-to-be-illegal alcohol. The main obstacle to the venture, strangely enough, proved to be Colosimo himself, happy in the wealth he had and wanting to settle down respectably with his young love, a singer named Dale Winter. Torrio would not let his partner's new morality stand in his way, and he hooked up with Capone on the potentially dangerous plan of killing Big Jim Colosimo. Capone's part was vital, for Torrio had to be seen to be absolutely innocent of the deed.

On May 11, 1920, Colosimo received a call concerning a truckload of whiskey that needed delivery. He went to his cafe to make arrangements, but he never left it. He was killed at close range by an unknown gunman—not surprisingly, since Capone arranged the hit through Frankie Yale in New York. It is possible that Yale himself was the killer.

The funeral was the first of the enormous affairs that would become the theater of gangland murders, with five thousand mourners in a mile-long procession. Torrio was now the head of one of the most powerful gangs in Chicago. His rapidly elevated lieutenant was, of course, Al Capone.

The Life and Times of

An illicit still dismantled during Prohibition

Capone's armored car

THE BUSINESS OF CRIME

John Torrio operated on a higher plane than the other Chicago gangs simply because of the scope of his vision. He saw the possibility of distributing liquor on a far wider scale than just his local powerbase, though he knew that success depended upon alliances with, or defeat of, other "bootleggers," as the makers or suppliers of illicit alcohol became known. His lead was one that Capone was bound to find attractive, so Al stayed where he saw the potential for profit, and he brought the rest of his family to Chicago. He was soon known as a subtle yet brutal character, and became involved in several areas of Torrio's network, from brothels to the motor pool. He was relied upon to control other wayward gang members and was said to have strangled several double-dealing hoodlums to death.

The opposition to Torrio's systemized criminal network came less from the establishment than from the other gangs. Payment to officials was already taken for granted in the city, and Torrio's belief in the advantages of peace for profit gave him sway with the political leaders, whose reelection chances depended upon the outward upholding of that same peace. Mayor William Hale Thompson was given large sums of money to continue to overlook corruption in Chicago, and the payouts continued all the way down to the street cops. Torrio showed political foresight when he helped the governor of Illinois, Len Small, to contest charges of corruption in 1921; a little judicious bribery and a few threats got Small acquitted and set Torrio up with an ally whose protection was worth much more than the few thousand dollars he had paid out. By the time he was twenty-three, Al Capone was near the top of an organization offering profitable business with a guarantee of noninterference by the authorities. He was on a healthy percentage of Torrio's prostitution and bootlegging profits, and two years later would be a multi-millionaire.

Although his criminal education was fast teaching him to control the temper that had already gotten him into trouble, Capone was still liable to fly off the handle for no particular reason. One public example occurred during 1922 when, while driving some friends around town, he crashed into a parked taxi. Capone exploded with rage at the innocent cab driver, pulled out a deputy sheriff's badge, and shoved a gun against the man's head, threatening to kill him. The police arrived and threw him in jail, though no charges were brought.

On the whole, however, Capone was gaining in wisdom. Torrio's distribution network brought about alliances with the majority of Chicago's gangs, and included the division of the city into areas agreed between them. The strongest of his rivals was the northside gang led by Charles Dion O'Banion, a jovial, calculating killer whose henchmen included Earl "Hymie" Weiss, Vincent "The Schemer" Drucci, Louis "Two Gun" Alterie, and George "Bugs" Moran. Bizarrely, O'Banion's chief delight was flower arranging; his flower shop, Schofield's, became the only place for gangsters to order wreaths after a murder. Other gangs, like those of the six Genna brothers, the southside O'Donnells (no relation to the westside O'Donnells), the Sheldons, and "Polack" Joe Saltis, joined in with Torrio's combine. In a perfect world Torrio would have been able to sit back and listen to the ring of cash registers—as he said, there was

The Life and Times of

plenty of action for everyone. But his new associates were not the most trustworthy of partners.

In 1923 Mayor Thompson was ousted from office by William Dever, who instituted a policy of closing illegal bars. He refused all attempts at bribery, and Torrio became seriously worried about the drying up of his outlets. In the spring Torrio himself was arrested after a raid on one of his illicit breweries and was saved from a conviction only by the fact that this was—ostensibly—his first offense. His troubles persuaded Spike O'Donnell of the southside O'Donnells to break the alliance, and O'Donnell started to strong-arm his way into Torrio's bars, beating up those who refused to change brands of beer. Torrio was forced to assert the unity of the combine, and arranged the killings of several of O'Donnell's "persuaders," though no one was charged because the gangsters' code of silence left the police with no evidence to make a case.

Frank McErlane, a member of the Saltis gang, was of increasing value to the combine as a hit man. Described as "the most brutal gunman ever to pull a trigger in Chicago," he was one of the few accurate shots in any of the gangs, and had been part of the team asserting Torrio's power over O'Donnell. McErlane was responsible for the attack on an O'Donnell liquor convoy, aimed at disrupting the southside gang's distribution network. His sharpshooting skills were unnecessary on this occasion (which was, in fact, the case in most mob killings, since most were carried out at very close ranges), as he forced the convoy drivers into his car and despatched them with a shotgun blast from the front seat. There was a general consensus among the other gangs that it was Capone who was behind the organization of the hit squads. Torrio's reputation was that of a peaceable hoodlum, whereas Capone was considered to be vicious and bloodthirsty. "That Capone kills like a beast in the jungle," complained Dion O'Banion.

To circumvent the new mayor's crackdown, Torrio sent

Capone to the suburb of Cicero, where the county sheriff was on the mobsters' payroll. The powers of the local police were ineffectual in the face of Torrio's superior clout, and the Cicero area soon became a Torrio-Capone stronghold. Cicero's Hawthorne Hotel became Capone's headquarters, from where he kept an eye on the local gambling joints and bars. His relationship with the local council was so profitable that he determined to make sure that its leaders were successful in the 1924 elections. His henchmen made the run-up to polling day a nightmare for Democrat candidates, and the polling stations themselves became the focus for threats and beatings. By the time special police forces had been transported from across the city boundary into the suburb it was too late, and the Republicans swept back into power. In the main shooting incident of the election, however, Capone's brother Frank was killed by the police. Frank and his fellow hoods mistook the plainclothesmen for opposing gang members, and he suffered a fatal gunshot wound in the chest. His funeral was a $20,000 affair, and was marked by a two-hour closing of the Cicero bars.

The result of the Cicero election was a free rein for Capone. Ironically, the suburb became an area almost free of petty crime, since the fear of retribution from Capone's enforcers was a greater threat than that inspired by the more usual legal powers. Cicero made Capone his fortune. Torrio cut him in for 50 percent of the takings, most of which could never be assessed.

Capone's control of the area also gave him the chance to show his mettle outside the shadow of Torrio's protective wing. He had learned his lessons well, and dealt with many of his problems without using violence. But no one was by now unaware of the savage temper under the businesslike manner, and Capone was not above dealing personally with those who stepped out of line. He gave the district something to think about in May 1924, as well as dispensing a lesson in loyalty to his men, when Jack Guzik, a junior and unpopular gang member, was beaten up by another underworld small-timer, Joseph Howard. Capone went straight to the bar where Howard was drinking and blew the top off Howard's head with six rounds. Two witnesses said they would identify Capone in court, and he went into hiding for a month. After he returned and handed himself in to the police there was an official inquest, by which time the witnesses had been struck with what Dion O'Banion used to call "Chicago amnesia." Guzik became a loyal follower of Capone, and achieved increasing importance as his business manager.

While Capone was out of town, Torrio got stung by O'Banion. The latter's unpredictability was what made him such a dangerous adversary, for his reaction was never guaranteed. He had killed two fellow hoods, the Miller brothers, in a crowded street for no particular reason that even he could think of, but he was just as capable of acts of generosity to strangers. That same May, O'Banion declared that he was ready to retire to a ranch in Colorado if Torrio would buy him out of his brewery for half a million dollars. They arranged to meet at the site, which was too large to be unknown to the police; in fact, a couple of officers were lounging around that morning, and the beer trucks usually had a police escort to save them from being ambushed. O'Banion, however, had gotten wind of a raid ordered by the police chief, and timed Torrio's arrival with that of the task force. Four hundred and fifty barrels of beer were impounded, the two officers had their badges ripped off their uniforms, and the two gang leaders were arrested. O'Banion was guaranteed to get off with a fine for his first offense, but it was Torrio's second. Not only that, but he had already paid O'Banion for an operation that the police had now closed down. As far as Torrio was concerned, O'Banion had overreached himself.

The city was quiet for several months, though a head of steam was building up within most of the gangs. The Genna brothers were itching to get their hands on O'Banion, to pay him back for his encroachments on their territory, as well as for personal insults that Torrio had smoothed over. Torrio was worried that a gang leader might be killed, and about the warfare that would ensue, but by November he was prepared to suffer an inevitable police clampdown if it meant getting rid of the O'Banion menace.

The thirteenth of November was the day of Mike Merlo's funeral. As the head of Chicago's Unione Siciliana, he had enormous influence with the town's underworld, and $100,000 worth of flowers were ordered for the cortège—most of them from O'Banion's flower shop. Three days before the funeral, three men came in to the shop to collect a $2,000 flower arrangement. One of them greeted O'Banion, shook hands with him, and kept a tight hold as the others pulled out guns and shot him six times. The men ran out to a car, which was protected by five other vehicles blocking the surrounding streets, and made their getaway.

The police got nowhere with their enquires. The two gunmen were from the Genna gang—no witness would want to identify them and appear in public again, though O'Banion's lieutenants knew who they were. The third man, who remained a mystery to all present, was Frankie Yale. Capone had used their firm friendship once again to give himself and Torrio a cast-iron alibi. Yale, who was known to the police, was questioned by them, but of course, as he said, he was in town for Mike Merlo's funeral, not O'Banion's.

Al Capone might escape police action following the murder, but Hymie Weiss and his colleagues weren't hamstrung by legalities, and they knew who pulled the strings behind the sort of meticulously planned attack that had killed their leader. In January 1925 Capone's car was forced off the road and raked with gunfire. By luck, the three men in the car escaped with their lives—Capone himself had not even been traveling in it. He took the hint, however, and ordered a steel-armored car that weighed seven tons.

That same month, Torrio was given ten days to settle his

affairs before starting a nine-month jail term. On January 24 he returned home after a shopping expedition with his wife and was attacked outside his front door by Hymie Weiss, Vincent Drucci, and Bugs Moran. Torrio fell with five bullets in him, though Moran never made his planned finishing-off shot as the hammer of his gun fell on an empty chamber; he had no time to reload, for the signal came to make a get-away. Torrio was rushed to hospital, where Capone dashed as soon as he heard the news. The wounded man refused to identify his attackers—even Capone was suspected, and was held overnight by the police for questioning. Two unidentified men attempted to gain access to Torrio, so Capone added his men to the police guard placed around the hospital room. Three weeks later, Capone took Torrio out of the hospital down a back stairway and got him safely to jail to begin his sentence, which, all in all, was about the most secure place in which he could recuperate.

Torrio's experience convinced him to retire as a gangster. With the guarantee of a percentage of his gang's income, he handed leadership over to the twenty-six-year-old Capone, together with an estimated gross annual revenue of $50 million and the prospect of an all-out fight for control of the city.

Michigan Avenue, Chicago

TAKING CONTROL OF A CITY

Capone wanted a friend, Tony Lombardo, a respected businessman, to take over as head of the Unione Siciliana, to keep political leverage in favor of his gang. The Genna brothers, however, had been strengthening their local position and wanted the power to move into other territories. One of them, Angelo, was pushed into the position of head of the Unione, and Capone suddenly found he needed to control the Gennas' increasing power. He arranged Angelo's roadside shooting in May 1925, making it look like a killing by the O'Banion gang. That assumption led to a spate of killings between the two gangs—O'Banion's and the Gennas'—which left two more of the Genna brothers dead and two arrested. Their organization had been cut off at the head and Lombardo was duly made the boss of the Unione Siciliana. Capone relocated his headquarters to the center of Chicago, a more fitting location for a citywide player.

Taming one gang, which was in any case supposed to be a Capone ally, did not bring peace to the underworld. Torrio had been right to get out when he did. Killings became an everyday occurrence, ping-ponging between gangs, as greed led to encroachment on territory, encroachment to murder, and murder to reprisal. Chicago soon became an American gangland talking-point; even Lucky Luciano, New York's mob supremo, thought the city was "a damned crazy place."

Frank McErlane brought a new level of madness to Chicago when, in September, he became the first to make use of John T. Thompson's lethal invention in an attempt to murder Spike O'Donnell. The Thompson submachine gun had gone into manufacture too late for use in the First World War, and was still almost unheard of six years later. It was the ideal weapon for the average off-target gangster, with a nominal rate of fire of a thousand rounds per minute, though McErlane's debut with the gun, which failed to kill O'Donnell, did cause some confusion—one report treated the neat line of bullet holes as a coincidence of shooting by a squad of gangsters. Capone seized on the potential of what became known as the "Chicago typewriter" or "Chicago piano," and ordered samples for himself and his men.

Al Capone spent Christmas of 1925 in New York, where he repaid Frankie Yale by taking charge of the nightclub killing of three of Yale's enemies, all of whom died in a hail of bullets. Capone was arrested with the men he had brought with him, but the problems of evidence were as great for the New York police as for those in Chicago, and Capone walked free on his story of having gone into the place for a quiet drink.

He returned to Chicago knowing that he had to deal with William "Klondike" O'Donnell, leader of the westside O'Donnells, who had been forcing his beer on Capone's bar owners. The loss of prestige could be more important than the loss of a few bars. After hitting on a couple of minor gang members, Capone went for Klondike and his top gunmen in April 1926. By the time the hit took place, however, Klondike had been dropped off at his house. Capone was one of four machine-gun handlers who sprayed Klondike's car with bullets, killing his brother, Myles O'Donnell, and a hit man, James Doherty, as well as a minor player, Thomas Duffy. What Capone had not bargained for was the additional presence in the car of Bill McSwiggin, a prominent assistant state attorney.

McSwiggin's death brought about an unprecedented crackdown on crime in Chicago. The fact that he had been in the company of known villains when he died was explained by a story about the recovery of a bullet-proof vest from his corpse; it was not revealed, however, that he and Doherty had been friends since school. Although there was nothing with which to charge Capone, the authorities were certain that he was behind the killings. He was once again forced into hiding, and his various premises were ransacked and closed down. Chicago came as close as it ever would to becoming dry.

Capone kept his head low until July, when he handed himself over to the police, determined not to get trapped in any unofficial retaliation by McSwiggin's colleagues. He walked free after three days, swearing by the friendships he had had with the dead men.

As far as the O'Banion gang was concerned, Hymie Weiss was the natural choice as leader of the men left at the top. They were united by their desire to see Capone cut down, and set a plan in motion soon after he returned from hiding. His driver was kidnapped and murdered, presumably after having been forced to give up information about his boss's routine.

In September they struck, with a daylight raid against the Hawthorne Restaurant, a habitual lunch spot for Capone. He was sitting with his bodyguard Frank Rio when a car raced by, chattering machine guns firing at the crowded restaurant. Strangely, no damage was done. Rio guessed it was a ruse, and dragged Capone to the floor as ten cars rounded the corner at an almost stately pace, this time with gunmen firing bullets rather than blanks. The first attack had been designed to draw Capone out of the restaurant, and it had nearly worked. The restaurant was devastated by the attack, and several people were wounded, but there were no fatalities. Capone helped to pay for hospital treatment and repairs; this was his neighborhood and he held a respected local position.

He denied that there was a war going on, insisting on his desire for peace, but he had been hit in his heartland and his prestige demanded a reaction.

Early in October he set up a stakeout in rooms around Schofield's flower shop, in a plan that called for both patience and alertness. A week later, on October 11, Weiss and four henchmen approached the shop on foot after driving from Joe Saltis's trial, which Weiss had promised to fix. The hidden gunmen opened fire, catching the north-siders in a crossfire that pockmarked the street. Weiss and one other person were fatally wounded. A list bearing the names of the Saltis trial jurors was found in Weiss's pocket, and at his apartment the police found another list, this time of witness names. In the aftermath, Capone expressed his lack of surprise at Weiss's death, explaining that he had begged various gang leaders to run their business on peaceful lines. His alibi was irrefutable, as usual—all the police could do was be thankful that there was one fewer gangster on the street.

It had been almost two years since the attack on John Torrio, twenty-one months of killing and counter-killing, with the forces of law and order standing off for the most part. When the smoke cleared, Al Capone was the man left standing. The northside gang, formerly O'Banion's and now led by Bugs Moran, sued for peace, and a meeting was convened at which the gang leaders decided upon an amnesty and a return to territorial boundaries. There were several isolated incidents, but Capone was now strong enough to make the other leaders keep to their decision to stop the wars.

A Chicago street market

The Palm Island house

"THE MAYOR OF CROOK COUNTY"

At the end of 1926, Bill Thompson announced his return to the candidature for the next mayoral elections. His pre-election promise was to make wet all that Mayor Dever had dried up, and as a result, the bootlegging community was extremely generous with its gifts to party funds, and with persuasion. Thompson returned to office with a large majority, not all of which had needed to be enforced by gangland pressure—Chicago loved Thompson's populist stand; it considered itself to be an open city and had never asked for prohibition.

Al Capone was now awarded almost celebrity status. Not only did he have real clout with the mayor's office, but his presence was something that gave any occasion a frisson of excitement and danger. His imposing bulk and his surprisingly cultured, confident conversation found him invitations into areas of society normally closed to street villains. Above all, Capone's power and wealth were by now too great for his bloody ascent to be remarked upon. In addition, his attendance at any public event was a guarantee that it would be trouble free. He was open about his business, and admitted that he was a bootlegger; as he pointed out, however, the parties he gave and attended were full of people eager to consume his product. He could easily afford the life of a celebrity. An estimate put the gross income from all his business interests in 1927 at $100 million. His employees were well paid, his wardrobe was extensive, and his personal wealth was thought to be $3 million. He could afford to lose single bets of $50,000 at the racetrack, and would pick up the drink tab for a whole club when the fancy took him. His attention to the poor of Chicago—buying fuel in winter, opening soup kitchens, and so on—combined with individual acts of generosity, made him, in the eyes of many, a romantic outlaw figure, even years after his fall.

In his home he was very much the family man. He doted on his children, he cooked, he appeared at the door in his slippers. Still, however much he may have accepted the trappings of the social A-list, his past was one that was bound to come up and meet him again.

The remaining fragments of the Genna gang were picked up by Joseph Aiello, a small-time northside boss with a grudge against Capone for getting Tony Lombardo made head of the Unione Siciliana. Aiello first offered Capone's chef $10,000 if he would lace the latter's food with prussic acid. This failed attempt was followed with a bounty offer of $50,000 to anyone who could kill Capone. There were ten attempts on Capone's life during 1927, all of which were stopped by Capone's hit men, and ended in funerals for the bounty hunters. During November police information led to the discovery of several ambush points set up by Aiello, obviously planned to take out the "Mayor of Crook County," as Capone was sometimes known. Aiello was brought in for questioning, and a group of Capone's men surrounded the police station. They were disarmed by the police and locked in cells close to Aiello, from where they passed enough threats to make him promise to give up his offensive.

Although Chicago society feted the gang boss, the city authorities were beginning to put the pressure on. Mayor Thompson had hopes of running for president, but his status as mayor of Capone's town was not one likely to win him the nomination. Capone decided to spend some time in Florida, where corruption was at a high enough level for gambling joints and bars to run successfully, until the heat died down. He first went on a train ride to Florida's west coast, but received such short shrift from the police department there that he moved on. His return to Chicago was met with antagonism; he was threatened with arrest every time he left his house, and was soon on his way back to Florida.

More harassment greeted him in Miami, but he quietly bought a sumptuous complex on Palm Island and began a $100,000 renovation. He was in Chicago to witness the failure of Thompson's nominations for the council in the April 1928 elections, amid a wave of bombings against both Republicans and Democrats. It appeared that the voters had had enough of flagrant lawlessness. Capone's business interests were safe in the hands of his subordinates, so he traveled back to his Florida retreat.

The rest of 1928 brought Capone more trouble, however. He had discovered that Frankie Yale was double dealing him on the protection of his beer trucks through New York, and decided therefore to have his old friend and mentor killed. On July 1, Yale was tricked out on to the road by a false message about the health of his new wife. He was attacked by several unknown killers, who made sure of their victim, downed in the initial onslaught, with a .45 slug to the head. Before the year's end, Yale's colleagues had struck their first note of revenge by killing Tony Lombardo. His successor, Pasqualino Lolordo, another friend of Capone, was gunned down in his own home four months later by members of Bugs Moran's northsiders. Moran was gaining in confidence, and Capone set Frank "The Enforcer" Nitti, one of his top killers, on to a plan to remove the northside boss. Nitti was responsible for the gang's internal discipline; with Capone increasingly spending time away from Chicago, Nitti became his natural number two.

Capone's own health also suffered during the year. He

contracted syphilis from a woman he had installed at his headquarters hotel; she sought a doctor's advice, but he, apparently, did not. And at the end of the year he caught the flu, which turned into double pneumonia. He was up and about by the end of January 1929, but had to take life easy around his Florida estate. In Chicago during early February, Capone's men rented several rooms around the SMC Cartage Company, in a pattern that had become almost a trademark beginning to an attack. SMC was Moran's bootlegging head-quarters, and the trap was set around the offer of a truckful of good-quality whiskey that Moran needed, after a failed attempt by him to sell a cheaper brand to his bars.

There were seven northsiders at the garage where the supposed whiskey deal was to take place on the morning of February 14, St. Valentine's Day, including Moran's "heav-ies," the Gusenberg brothers, as well as his accountant and a mechanic. The arrival of his brother-in-law, Albert Weinshank, caused Capone's lookouts to set the hit in motion, as Weinshank bore a likeness to Moran. Thus the main target, Moran himself, who was late, saw a detective car outside the garage and, not wanting to deal with some petty police wrangle, went to get a cup of coffee.

The car was, of course, not from the police department but had been made to look like one, and two of its five pas-sengers were dressed as uniformed officers. They entered the garage and, at gunpoint, ordered the gang members up against the wall. The three hit men stepped forward with submachine guns and shotguns and sprayed a withering fire back and forth along the line of men, causing several of them to be almost literally shot to pieces. As a final flourish, the squad left the garage in a manner designed to look as though the fake police were arresting the three gunmen.

By the time the real police had arrived on the scene the fake car was long gone. Miraculously, Frank Gusenberg was still alive—he had been standing on the end of the line and must have caught less of the fusillade. But even though his wounds were fatal he would not reveal the names of his killers. Moran was discovered hiding in a hospital, guarded by his henchmen and denying that he even knew the victims.

The St. Valentine's Day Massacre became a symbol of the cold violence of the Chicago underworld. Its ruthlessness galvanized the police into new levels of activity, yet, although they found the car and several witnesses, they had only speculation as to the actual perpetrators; for a time there was a rumor that the men in uniform actually were officers. Capone was brought up from Florida for questioning, but it was madness to imagine that he would offer any helpful information. In fact, the questions he was asked concerned his tax status as much as the massacre, a detail that would make sense in due course.

The St. Valentine's Day Massacre

A WEAPON AGAINST THE MOB

The shockwave from the St. Valentine's Day Massacre rever-
berated throughout America, causing consternation
amongst the criminal fraternity, which worried about a
national clampdown on its activities. In May 1929, therefore,
a national mobsters' convention met in Atlantic City, where
the crime bosses from around the country, chaired by the
gangsters' peace envoy, John Torrio, signed an agreement to
wipe the slate clean on former grudges. Capone had raced
there from a macabre banquet in honor of three men whom
he had discovered were plotting against him.

The latest head of the Unione Siciliana, Joseph Guinta,
had gotten the idea that he could take over from Capone,
and he had persuaded John Scalise and Albert Anselmi,
Capone's long-serving hit men, that they could profit by join-
ing him. Capone was deeply hurt by the betrayal when his
information network discovered the plot, and the banquet
had been planned as a lesson to the rest of the gang. Most
of the evening was a model of good cheer and fine food. But,
after the brandy had been served, Capone meted out the
punishment to Guinta, Scalise, and Anselmi himself with a
baseball bat, working himself into a frenzy with the ferocity
of the blows. The beaten traitors were then shot and their
bodies dumped several miles away.

The recent activity against him convinced Capone that he

needed to lie low for a time. He therefore came up with the idea of getting himself arrested on a minor charge, so as to draw a couple of months' safety in prison. On May 16, 1929, he and Frankie Rio arrived in Philadelphia and were spotted going into a theater by two detectives. They were arrested for carrying guns—something Capone had not done in a long time—and had no money on them with which to bail themselves out. The charges of "being a suspicious character and carrying a concealed weapon" were processed in less than a day, but the judge, seizing his opportunity, gave them a maximum sentence of a year in jail; the more usual punishment was a fine.

Capone and Rio began their term in Philadelphia's toughest prison, but were moved to a more lenient establishment. Shocked at the sentence, they began the first of six unsuccessful appeals, each backed up with generous financial inducements. Capone complained that he was being made a universal scapegoat for every wrong in America; "Tell them I deny absolutely that I am responsible," he cracked to his lawyer after the Stock Market crash of October 1929.

Capone and Rio were obliged to serve the full term, with two months' remission as model prisoners. The only break they were given was when they were moved secretly to another prison on the day before the release date of March 17, 1930, so as to avoid the five-hundred-strong crowd waiting for Capone to appear; the threat of an assassination attempt was a very real one.

By the time he got out of prison, the authorities had embarked upon a new plan to bring gangsters to justice. In October 1928 the Supreme Court had ruled that illegally earned income was taxable. The decision effectively meant that the Internal Revenue Service became the first line of attack against the underworld. Its Special Intelligence Unit began the painstaking work of leafing through bank records and information taken during police raids on illegal establishments to find proof of income that had not been declared

The Life and Times of

on gangsters' tax returns. As most such returns made piti-
fully small declarations, the team knew that there had to be
hidden resources that financed the gangsters' lifestyles; it
was a case of finding the chinks in their serpentine banking
procedures, and tracing false accounts back to their origin.

The powers of the IRS were applauded by the president,
Herbert Hoover, who felt a particular animosity toward the
symbol of gangland America, Al Capone. "Have you got
that fellow Capone yet?" became the president's daily
question to the Secretary of the Treasury.

As the Special Intelligence Unit began its work, its head,
Elmer Irey, soon realized that Capone would be a difficult
fish to land. He had covered his tracks effectively; officially
he owned very little, and he showed no visible income—he
had never paid income tax, so there was no previous stan-
dard of living against which to make a comparison.

However, the SIU did discover information about his
nearest associates that had not been buried deeply enough.
In the week of Capone's release from prison, Frank Nitti
was indicted on charges connected with two years' tax evasion, and the succeeding month saw Capone's brother
Ralph saddled with a three-year conviction. In November
Jack Guzik was sentenced to five years in prison for his
proven income imbalance. It was obvious from the senior
rank of the catch that the net was tightening around
Capone, but whether he would be able to slip through the
mesh was quite another thing.

Once out of prison, Capone found it difficult to find
a town in which he could move without being arrested.
The Chicago authorities made it plain that they didn't care
whether or not they had anything to charge him with, but
they would take him in anyway. Prohibition supervisor
Alexander Jamie had recently put Eliot Ness in charge
of a small group of incorruptible agents whose hard work
and moral integrity would win them the name
"Untouchables," though they did not in the end have a

hand in Capone's final downfall. In Florida the governor sent notes to his county sheriffs to arrest Capone on sight, and the gangster's estate there had already been raided. Florida might have accepted a certain relaxation of national laws, but it didn't want an outsider muscling in on home-grown corruption, especially one who didn't accept a dividing line between relaxation and abandonment of the law.

The situation with the IRS was immediately apparent to Capone, and he took advice from Torrio's tax specialist, Lawrence Mattingly. Mattingly arranged a meeting with the IRS to attempt to work out a voluntary payment. This was the usual way to avoid charges being brought in affairs of this kind. However, Mattingly failed to appreciate the importance of his client in the eyes of the IRS. They wanted Capone behind bars—the president wanted Capone behind bars.

He ignored the warnings to keep out of Florida, arriving in April 1930. He was soon to experience the first of four arrests, which signaled clearly the authorities' determination to carry out their threat to stop him from setting foot in Miami. He also had to fight an attempt to close his estate, which was said to be a haven for criminals and vagrants. Capone fought the first problem by suing for false imprisonment, and won an order preventing the police from arresting him on sight. The attempt to keep him out of his own home failed, as the judge stated that he could not expel a citizen simply because his presence in an area was not deemed suitable. Capone tried to counter the bad publicity with charitable donations and swimming parties, and it seemed that he had at least one base where he could show his face in public.

His Chicago operation, in the meantime, was carrying on very well without him. With periodic drops in income when a crackdown was launched, business carried on as usual. The killings were regular, but they now tended to be more personal than gang-based. When Capone began planning for

The Life and Times of

the end of prohibition he was ahead of many officials and politicians, who thought it was around for good. He would need to change direction, and was considering legitimate businesses as well as the more obvious option of union racketeering, of which he had some experience because of the need for the efficient transportation of alcohol.

The thought of directing his talents toward legitimate operations was attractive for the man whose popularity was always stained by the inevitable media image. Although he was the subject of worldwide interest, most of it was disparaging rather than admiring. It was not surprising that the thirty-one-year-old was tired of the constant vigilance needed to protect his person; he had done and witnessed things with which nobody who had any pretensions toward civilization would want to be faced.

Capone in court, 1931

GOING DOWN

The summer of 1930 tied two knots in the net that eventually caught Al Capone. Edward J. O'Hare was a lawyer-turned-bootlegger and dog-track entrepreneur who joined with Capone in order to extend his business. He did not see himself as part of the underworld, however, so when he came under investigation, he arranged a deal with the Special Intelligence Unit. Described as "the best stool pigeon the government ever had," his information led the SIU to various documents and papers that would help to prove that Capone did indeed have an income. The second "knot" was the fortuitous rediscovery by the authorities of books of account taken in a raid after the death of Bill McSwiggin, which had been considered useless at the time and had been forgotten. They gave details of certain gambling-joint profits between 1924 and 1926, and included an "Al" in the reckoning. The task was to prove that "Al" was Capone.

In the autumn Capone decided to risk a public backlash by killing Joe Aiello, who had succeeded to the leadership of the Unione Siciliana and was flexing new muscles against his old adversary. Once again, rooms surrounding the apartment of the victim were rented, and after ten days' vigilance Aiello made a target of himself when he got into a taxi outside the building. He was gunned down by two submachine guns fired from different windows. No arrests were made.

February 1931 saw Capone in court again, this time on a charge of contempt of court resulting from his late appearance in court to answer questions about the St. Valentine's Day Massacre. He had provided a doctor's affidavit stating that his pneumonia had prevented him from turning up on time, but he had been spotted around Miami looking fit and well at the time. The affidavit was shown to be false, and Capone was given a six-month prison sentence. No judge, presented with a guilty Al Capone in court, would award less than the maximum permissible sentence for even the most trifling offense.

The following month, however, brought the main thrust of the authorities' assault upon Capone, with the first indictment against him by U.S. Attorney General George Johnson. It was Johnson who, in 1928, had secured the services of the SIU for the specific purpose of bringing about Capone's downfall. The indictment was made in secret while others were prepared, though Capone's spy network was too wide-ranging for it to pass unnoticed.

By June there were twenty-three counts listed against Capone, alleging a total of over $200,000 in unpaid taxes. It was emphasized that these amounts bore no relevance to Capone's actual earnings, but that they were the sums on which the SIU claimed it could prove a tax liability.

On June 13, 1931, Capone pleaded guilty to all charges. He knew he would go to jail, but the expected term was no more than three years. The press described the probable outcome as a victory for the gangster. Before the sentencing on July 30, Capone declared that he would be turning to honest business after the affair was over.

When the court convened, Judge Wilkerson confounded both prosecution and defense by announcing that he would not be following the attorney general's usual recommendations about sentencing for tax evasion. George Johnson was forced to admit that the government and Capone's lawyers had between them worked out a guilty plea in return for a

The Life and Times of

relatively light sentence, during the time when the indictments were being prepared. The defense concurred with Johnson's belief that, had the judge's decision been known, Capone would have pleaded not guilty. The upshot was a withdrawal of the guilty pleas, and the setting of a new trial for October.

In the period before the second trial, Edward O'Hare informed the SIU that Capone was collecting the list of jurors' names in order to bribe and threaten them into a not-guilty verdict. As a result, Judge Wilkerson came up with the ploy of a last-minute switch with the jury from another case being tried at the same time. Capone came to trial in front of a set of unknown names.

The trial established that Capone received an income, called witnesses to testify to his "air of ownership" of premises that were not in his name, and gave detailed accounts of his spending on hotels, clothes, and gambling. The defense suffered from a lack of preparation for a plea of not guilty. They could not deny Capone's expenditure, but also could not prove that he had no income, whereas the prosecution, who technically needed to show Capone's income, gave overwhelming indication of it, if not the actual proof. The jury found Capone guilty on only five of the twenty-three counts, but Wilkerson awarded a maximum sentence of eleven years, together with nearly $80,000 in fines and costs; the sentence was to begin immediately. The most celebrated gang boss and murderer in the country was going to prison for tax evasion.

Capone spent seven months in the county jail, until all his appeals had finally been denied. He was sent to prison in Atlanta in May 1932, a carefully picked establishment with a tough reputation, and free of any of the accomplices with whom he might create a prison gang.

He was determined to show himself a model prisoner, in order to earn the maximum remission on his sentence. In March 1933, while he was learning to make shoes in one of the prison shops, the world outside was freed of prohibition by the repeal of the Volstead Act. Rumors circulated about Capone's special treatment while in Atlanta—he had access to expensive cigars and specially made shoes, and was also said to employ bodyguards—all of which were denied by the prison governor. However, Capone did manage to get money smuggled into the prison, and that fact was bound to give him an edge over the other $10-per-week prisoners. It was decided to close down every possible advantage to Capone.

In August 1934 he was among the first batch of prisoners transported to Alcatraz, a former army base set on a windswept rock, a mile and a quarter out to sea in San Francisco Bay. The regime was rigid. Prisoners were allowed almost no contact with the outside world, nor were they permitted any form of currency from which a position of power could be wrangled. Even tobacco, the traditional prison barter, was made worthless by being constantly available.

Capone's single-minded good behavior counted against him with those fellow inmates who had longer sentences, and thus less to lose. He was involved in several fights over trifling matters, and survived a scissor attack, and attempts at both poisoning and strangling him.

In February 1938 Al Capone suddenly developed symptoms of mental instability. He was found wandering around the prison in a confused state, and was soon raving and drooling. He was diagnosed as suffering from tertiary syphilis, the severe and uncommon stage of the disease he had contracted in 1928. Neurosyphilis was incurable, though it was controllable to an extent; he should have taken treatment soon after the original infection.

From now on, Capone would suffer a gradual deterioration of his mental powers, with periods of almost normal behavior interspersed with outbreaks of instability similar to the first one. He adopted the shuffling walk associated with the illness and spent the rest of his prison term in

The Life and Times of

the hospital. He was, however, happy, though sometimes disorientated—and his sentence was almost up.

Capone was released from Alcatraz on January 6, 1939, though obliged to serve a further year, less remission, in the county jail for his misdemeanor offenses. He became a free man on November 16 that year. A week before his final release, Ed O'Hare was gunned down in his car in Chicago. The criminal fraternity had served its own form of justice.

Capone spent four months in treatment at a hospital in Gettysburg before returning to Palm Island. He spent his remaining days there quietly with his wife and her relatives. While he played golf and went out to restaurants, the Treasury persisted with attempts to find assets in his name for them to claim against his back taxes. They found it impossible to find anything. Capone was not short of living expenses, but the money came out of nowhere. He continued to receive visits from the old gang in Chicago, who would satisfy his occasional delusions of being the head of the outfit. Jack Guzik, who was one of the regular visitors, once answered a reporter's question about Capone, saying, "Al? He's as nutty as a fruitcake."

On January 21, 1948, the forty-eight-year-old Capone suffered a massive brain hemorrhage, and was given the last rites by a priest. He regained consciousness, however, and was able to talk with his family. He caught pneumonia four days later and died of a heart attack on January 25. Few of his contemporaries had achieved such a peaceful end.

He was transported under some secrecy back to Chicago, and buried on February 4 in the presence of family and close friends. In 1950 his body was moved away from the sightseers, to an unpublicized spot in Mount Carmel Cemetery. On his tombstone, the inscription beneath his name reads "My Jesus Mercy."

INDEX

INDEX

Al Capone's wife, 1932